Fingers of Words

Selected Poems

(c) Jem Fell 2023

Jem Fell

1st Edition - 2022
2nd Edition (revised) - 2023

(c) Jem Fell

Published by Quords, Ipswich

Formatting, printing by Blurb

For Rachel,

Thank you for tolerating my explorations, my flights of fancy and for encouraging me and giving me the space to grow into x

Contents

A Corner

A little over a year ago I was idling about in a forest of notebooks and neglected filing, thinking about nothing in particular, but aware of how long it was since I'd written anything really. There were the odd words, a few scribblings in the margins of a café, but nothing you could in good conscience call writing. I started collating things together, read through all those things I'd written since the very first stanza slipped onto a page back in 1997 in the greyness of a Lancaster call centre – for they pretty much all exist, on my unedited hard-drive or in wild triplicate flurries of over-enthusiastic printouts teetering on the shelves below my desk. I read, and I gathered things together, and produced a little booklet to inflict on family at Christmas. They smiled and sidled off for a mince pie. Somehow in that moment of reflection on almost twenty-five years of writing, I realised there were words I liked, words that weren't the time-limited, self-indulgence I'd painted them as – it gave me a confidence boost. Always nice. I started to think about writing again, not in the oh-I-ought-to way, but as an actual focussed thought. The pen came out. The café was frequented. My eye wandered along streets. I had a loose theme in my head, a vague plan for 52 poems across the year. Not a target, but a loose aspiration. As long before though, I found that once the pen slipped nib across smoothed page the words surge forth, and by summer that aspiration was long reached.

Looking now, as I piece together this collection, not simply throwing poems in as I unearth them, I find there are other themes I've written about along with that early one. That made the structure of this collection relatively simple – I'm never that keen on chronology as an organisational tool. Far too coldly rational!

Going into 2023, I have a new theme, plans to perform, and the hope that last year's reviewing will mean this is the year the novel's lingering gestation finally moves forward. No targets, but maybe there'll be more words in 2024.

I do hope you enjoy these words.

JF Jan 2023

I've been writing poems for over twenty-five years, initially as a way of distracting myself from the tedium of sitting in a grey call-centre cubicle, then for myself, for performance, for catharsis, for friends. There have been hiatuses, I find it hard to write poetry whilst writing prose, but it's been a constant through all those years.

One of my endless frustrations as a writer is the presumption that my words are automatically autobiographical (good job I'm not a crime writer in that case), an assumption that people make especially about poetry. A fellow poet avoids that by writing about the natural world, but that's not my thing. I have tried, really, I have, I've got so much admiration for people who can versify greenfinches or dahlias, but I'm a responsive, emotional, poet. I write about moments in time. It's just that those moments in time aren't necessarily my moments in time.

Some poems clearly stem from personal experience, some don't, will you know? I don't know. I sort of hope not, because if it's obvious then doesn't that mean my writing's in some way different if it's not personal. Sometimes there's a kernel of experience, mediated through possibility, the creative vortex of might-have-been – imagination – how would things have been if I'd reacted differently. Some are imaginings in response to something seen, a couple, a moment of silence, a dash for a train... what's the story? Others are whimsy, flights of fancy, sat in Hullabaloo on a Saturday afternoon with my coffee and feta toastie allowing my pen to roam. Some of them are amongst my favourites. I do love a bit of flighty whimsy.

Finally, I don't follow all that teacherly advice to draft, redraft and redraft. Again, like the sparrows, I wish I could in many ways, but I find my poems feel dead when I return and pick at them, hone, craft. I write, long hand, with a lovely pen – it connects my thoughts to the paper in a beautiful way so my words flow down my inky arm onto the page – then I type them up. There's minimal tweaking in that, a word choice on line two, a comma, an and deleted in the final stanza, then done. If I don't like it, gone. Abandoned. I will use it maybe for parts, steal the line I like, but I'm absolutely a no redraft poet. Some may say, ha, we can tell. Cool, I'm not focused on form, I'm about emotion, rhythm, the movement, and above all, the way the words connect. To me. To the reader. To you.

On Writing

Nights Out

Thoughts

Looking for a way to choose poems for a recent performance, I discovered just how many of my poems have been inspired by nights out.

That shouldn't, perhaps, have been such a surprise, nights out are intrinsic to my well-being - the dance floor after midnight is where I come alive. It's more than that though, a night out carries with it narrative; the lead in, escalation, drama and the sunrise epilogue. There's the narrative of possibility, the strangers viewed for a fragment of a moment, gone into...What? the naked man many many years ago who ran past in Halifax after midnight shouting "you bastards" into the dark, surely deserves a poetic sequence of his own. There are the flirtatious in corners, the angry, the sad birthday celebrant crying in an alcove with their wilting balloon. Under cover of darkness, in glitter heels, our soul sings.

And I write.

Then there's the passing of time, the lost things. Yes, in part youth, and friends no longer on our journey, but also places. Places that held in their sticky carpets and sweaty walls the tales of regret, delight and passion, that made us feel safe, alive, connected. Places that are gone, places important to our own self-mythologising. Clubs, bars, university, queer spaces. A house party gate-crashed. The desperation at four in the morning to keep the party going even as the birds start to sing.

All of that, and perhaps especially the lost spaces, deserve to live on, not to be abandoned and forgotten as ephemeral. If a transient moment on a hillside hearing a warbler can be inspirational, I'm absolutely sure that lifting your arms to Soft Cell on a stage in a crowd of friends is so much more so.

Alive

Cascading with delight into nights
A fidgeting vortex of thrumming energy
Leaping in gregarious gusto from days
To feed dark ceaseless shots of life.

Unfiltered, sweeping away littoral drifted
Sandy spits of accumulated caution;

Choose - dance it, shout it, sing, live it,
Zero fucks, for today's the shot to down.

Grasp a gaze, hold attention's glitter
Leap with life's lust upstairs two-by-two
Across dance-floors, flick open bars
With a skip, a tempting plea. And

A toe steps with waking urgency
Resonating through rhythmic knee nudges
Ferments of hands winding fingers of words
Beneath tables that leap with conversation

That darting inquisitive lust for moments,
Seconds, people, things, thoughts,
Kisses the nights with ceaseless hints
Pockets of fabulous smiling tomorrows.

Dance floor

Bounding in steps of two
In giggles of stumbles, of a night
Alive through swing doors and
Sticky floors at the midnight moment,
Gin moment, the tequila moment,
Shots lined, a double of flushed faces,
Eyes turned, brushing, to the intensity
Of colour, timeless, fleeting, ephemeral.
In this moment, this lost moment,
Turning in a stumble of skin tight arms,
We are alive, you and me, in this
Glitter sheen of nothing, everything.

And we dance, oh we dance, immune.
In thighs, in elbows, in rivulets of dreams
Eyes held faster than shapes thrown in strobe.
We dance as one, inside each other's skin,
Your gaze kisses mine and we are alive,
With knees Bending, back thrown, rising
On waves of rhythm, centred in the tonight.

Fingers in fingers, eyelash tight, we are the
night
The streets and stairs, stars and 4am kerbs,
We are the sparkling kiss of the dance floor.

A Corner

Fuck, and in the twitch
Of facial hair,
Lost in the moustache's clip
Drawn in on dancing eyes
In the dark throb of three am

To this tight squeezed corner

Pressed

Hard to the wall by the
                Plant
                Dance-floor
                Bar

And tight to the bristle
Of confidences on tongues

Pocket tight
                Whisper close

                On lips.

Gin Nights

Glasses in the sky
    Of the one AM gin hour,
On a tide of exaltation
    In a nail's glitter
And in the smiled greeting
    Of this dancing place,
    Gin place, happy space,
With a flick of dried lime
    A twist of tonic's fizz
    The pour of the held gaze
    Folds these flighty feet
    Into hedonism's caress.

Corners, tables, teetering balance stools
We're in the heedless hours
The stretching envelope time
Warmly vanishing unseen

Dark, DJ time, shot time
Folding in beneath gregarious ferns

To conversational sip-smiles
Shared in teasing thefts

Flitting in the folds of bars

And there's this inching
Slow drawing together
            Of
            Feet
            Elbows
            Eyes

An imperceptible fusion of arms

The scarce heard word of smiles
Drift like shouts on bass beat whispers
Sparkling in transcendent shadows
And as glasses disappear
Ears consume the breath of thoughts

With the provocative squeeze
Of a hand abandoned in the dark

Lingering below belt loops...
And stepping in the shrinking duet bubble
Toecap close, nose close, thought close

A provocation of touches cascade
Ephemeral between verses

Ephemeral

The echo of choruses

Resonate through feet to invitations
Of touched lips

And the tight delightful arse-pull
Squeezed in this heedless corner
In the dark

And then, with the folding down of tunes
The final vodka sips, the seeping away,

A drift of regrets on farewell lips
To wander with the dreams of ah and gone

Leaving lips. Touch. Caress, linger. Arse. Eyes.
And
Gone.

Sunday Morning

Stumbling home in late night almost dark,
No, footsteps in the shadow of almost light,
The sheen of dancing still smiling through us
On the weaving hill of privet sleep;
Arms stretch in kerbside reprise,
Ear-ringing in still note-imperfect recollection
Of hedonistic, pirouetting, heedless flirtation
And there, there, you are, stretching
Across dawn's asphalt dance-floor
To pull me cornerward in a giggle
Of discordant steps, tumbling in improvisation
From kerb to slab to wall, gate
To sentinel lamp-post firm on the brow
And in the waning of that lonely light
You take me from the floor, still my beating feet
And with curling fingers, tongues knowing
All the moves, against the gate's rigid bars,
We rehearse the Ballad of Sunday Morning.

Gone into the warm mists of memory,
All those slicky-carpet playlists
Recollections of illicit toilet passion
Snogs, shapes and spilled drinks,
slipping into ethereal anecdote
like the sorrow of a dripping wall

dark, scratched, forgotten at six am...

Ah, these places, these spaces,
The Alex, The Bear...
Olivia's, Cindy's...
Dove, Rose, Betty's, Casey's...
The After Party, Brooks...

We danced, kissed, flirted with abandon,
Sat in sodden tears by swinging doors,
Leapt in sweat to every tainted tune,
Bounded in stairs of boisterous hedonism,
Downed shots of the never-ending night
Lingering on these, our stages of friendship,
Way beyond the strobe's final farewell
Kerb dancing our stumbling farewells

We threw passion into the night, span,
Hooked, made out, snogged, groped;
We twirled, sobbed, fought our dramas,
Ran, skipped, leapt, giggled and laughed.

In those lost jeans, steps, the arses felt,
The tongues waltzed, the hedonistic hands
In those midnight hours, lost hours,
Fragmentary speeding hours of seconds,
There, our glorious freedom of belonging,
Our space, mayfly fleeting, lost, forgotten,
But,
In those infinite fleeing seconds
There lay the throbbing beat of being
In the dancing safety, our space
Lost. Needed.

Lost Spaces

Summer

Missed Summer

I want hibiscus hedges
            Jupiler and cicadas
I want too hot afternoons
            Shade chasing for respite
Thimbles of coffee watching
            The louchely beautiful
The morning Le Monde amble
            Baguettes
            Gauloise Blondes
            Flaking croissants
Want the payage speed drop
            Bonjour bonsoir café nods
Want the right of the road
To joke about the wrong cheeses
            Lust for gleaming patisserie
Wake too early in sweating heat
            Vineyards
            Cascading heedless from hills
            Tabacs
            Boulangeries, shuttered streets
            Scuttling
            Golden cockroaches, lantern lit
A summer, a Gallic summer. Summer.

Ridges of thoughts
Moist with memory,
The gust of possibility
A breath upon my lobe,
Summer day caresses
Of lingering heat.

Like toes worming
Into tide damp sands

Sun kissed, breeze kissed,
Blushing in warmth's languor

To sip, tongue rolling
Across the hard elusive

Pleasure of lip held ice-cube

Bench sprawled in decadence
To capture the hints

Of wind's botanic kiss
Along thigh's lazy sheen,

Late July lounging
Lingers in
tongue rich depths.

Heat

Glistening with Gallic sunshine kisses,
Languidly spread on bank's grass,
Lake glimmering in still rippled air

Starfishing in avoidance of
Afternoon's lingering heavy press

Toes, limbs, mind, spread wide
As moor hens, heron, dragonflies, pass

Eyes closes, stilled in your heat,
Glittering breaths summer shallow

A delicate breeze, whisper soft
Kisses the heated blush of skin

Drawing the nub of delicious shivers,
Eyes closed in the soporific embrace
Of this endless French lover's afternoon

Spring Days

A spring day's dalliance perhaps
With the sliding of underwear
In the flowering meadows of our minds,
Thighs kissed with gin dashed lips
Skin flushed in primrose bed reflection
Folding in firm hand's exploration
As apple trees bud in soft blossom's blush
Slipping to grassy warmth's embrace.
Layers discarded with winter
The tantalising touch of temptation
Drawn on through every undulation,
With birdsong loud comes desire's sigh
For the length of summer's longing.
A dalliance of desire in the lee
Of summer's coyly lingering flirtation.

Sultry Night

Horny with sweat
Beneath the canvas,
Lewd imaginings of crickets
Your jazz-funk earworm.

Too hot, too hot;
Let's starfish in the dark,
Finger sketch dreams
On each other's skin -

Of breezes, cool breaths
From toe to hip to nipple

And kiss, kiss, lick, drink
In lingering caresses
Your salty exhalations.

Paddling

Yesterday it was I went paddling
at the foot of the deep ravine,
picnicking in the fern frond's soft arms;
plunging deep into the heady pool,
the warmth of spring on my back
as glistening delight adorned my face,
droplets of timeless wonder dripping
from the shapely rounded rocks swelling
forth, moss laden, succulent undulations
shielding my diving wonderment
from the tender ministrations of time.
Unhindered, sated, an afternoon pooled
When, paddling spent, I lay back to gaze,
Doze, beneath skies streaming blue hues.

The World

There's a pocket of time, of youth,
Of Merchants catching Witches on
The water of old John, gaunt,
Well Stoned, of Alex, sweaty in the dark/

Of squashed memory, the best bits,
Vivid; distant sunrises recalled
In effervescent friendly hues.

The drinks, borrowed signage
Keep off the Grass lounge warnings,
Hallway slug trail incense of ideals,
Midnight candle bound in
Attic dark Scarborough Fair complicity.

A moment more alive in time,
Alight with joy than the press
Of all those rolled years since,
Years amplifying the echoes
Cavorting in abandon to
Tainted Love, throw hands skyward
And, don't ever Sit Down.

And in this pocket, this crafted fragment
We step again in the dark hours
Along the dread Bishop's rise at 3am

Pump Shine on You Crazy Diamond,
New Generation to the door-propped corridor,
Beats blending in a waft of smoke
Escaping ageless down the years
A haze of youth on the breeze of memory

Remember when we were young?

And, for a moment of reconnections
A blink of a dance-floor held pint
A laugh, hug, handshake, a wish held
Thirty years in the bold insecurity of youth
Finally freed in delight of friends found anew

Reunion

Out of time, kissed in the moonlight of decades,
Once more flicking midnight ash away
In grassy circles of heedless cans and music
As lights flick away, floor to floor...

And we're momentarily ageless is this
Pocket of time, dreaming dreams
As sun rises across the Bay, of this place,
These people, these friends, this family,
Embracer of dreams, then, now, again.

Pyjama Hatred

Simply a Babygro, no more,
The bafflement of adults dressing
For bed is beyond me
-           Honestly, winceyette isn't winsome
Surely bedclothes are like bedtimes
A relic of youth's restrictions

Warmth is in a duvet
Warmth is in a lingering hug
Warmth is the foot fold
There's the warmth
Buttoned, barriered, to the lover's touch
Shielded from the sheet's caress
Hidden from the moon's lingering glance

Take the brushed cotton
Fit only for hotels or family visits
With their midnight landing dashes
A functional abomination

Wrap yourself side to side
Front to back
Arm, hand, leg, thigh and chest

Exalt in the kiss of fresh bedding
A lover in the dark
Leave the nightwear folded.
Dream naked.

Saturday Nights

A solitary night of echoed documentaries,
Sport's incessant cacophonies
Or darkly lonely B films
Stretch
With silent screams
Through futile hours
To an unsatisfied duvet

Out, with screening pint and pen
The papered alone is differently hued now,
The soft pinks of quiet musings,
Harsh monochromes
Stumbling upon the brashly youthful
Party hole
Barbed russets of courtyard groups
Oblivious in their frivolity

Yearning for that camaraderie
Giggles ringing from half-drunk glasses
The hedonism of sharing
The soft touch of a word's hand

In absence there are moments on paper,
Dreams and thoughts,
Rife in vibrant possibility
Smiling, comfortable with
Imagination's bright companionship –

Yet yearning echoes in sips
In pen strokes and breaths.

Silence

In theory, I understand
The silence thing. I do.
I get reflection,
Appreciate birdsong and wind
Know the power of calm
Less can be more
Even heard myself say
How nice, to sit together
In companionable silence
But.
But.
Silence explodes my head
Bursts eardrums
With it cacophony of nothing
I need cafés for writing
Chatter to think
The beat of conversation
The thrum of giggled trivia

Words. Noise. Bustle, people, ideas...
Libraries kill with whispers,
Instrumentals the soul stranglers
Silence destroys, squeezes life
A screaming deathly oppression.
Profound, inconsequential,
Soft or loud, I don't care,
Just take this fucking silence
And fill my heart, ears and mind
With swirling spoken words.

Cacophony

In the sun, the wash of waves
A soporific rhythm to the endless
Banality of overheard conversation.

Work and weather, the utter
Tedium of Carol's tribulations
And a thousand unpicked ailments,

I find myself unfeasibly
Intolerant of these inconsequences,
Trivia laced with nipping teeth

Until, with Tony's marital foibles
Ripping a hole in my mind,
I drain my mug and just flee

Crisp November night's greeting
Stepping alone into grouped gathering
The scrunch of discomfort
Gravels beneath party feet
Glittering tentative in unknown knots;
Pitchers of Estrella gradually fold me
Into gregariousness' rambling warmth.
Tumbling at anointed ten from outside
To drift nooked corner, table to table
Rounds flowing like Aran yarn's warmth
Until
In stepped gathering of reluctant partings
We linger in the late locked lamplight
Loitering in pavement pauses
For the departure's embrace
And
Initially uncertain   again
The night welcomes weaving eager steps
Highway striding, arm in arm
Of interlinked fingers of conversation
Down, round, up, steps spilling the light
Of anticipation into the midnight hours
To be
Greeted in bafflement, flowing down

Stairs
Steep to basement kitchen, garden – gin
Glasses filled and foraging for speakers,
Tinsel adorned, clad in bear hugs
Floorboards and fruit bowl embellished
With light dancing steps of friendship
Swaying
Though landings, in star and fridge-light
Until
At four, five, sunrise, the night's kissed farewell
Slipping away to swift slumbers
Warmed in thought and weary musing
Of gleaming birthday hours well worn.

Competitive words linger long
Like Grandma's overcooked Sunday beef
So many manners posturing for place
Between silently clustered assumptions
Lurking between cutlery's IKEA gaps.

Assumptions direct the friendly chatter
With posturing miasma undercurrents
Barriers of decorum tether conversation
To the safety of scripted provocation's tedium –
Serious role-play at light-hearted toil.

Dinner?

Please spare me from the casually indifferent aperitif,
Distract me from heartfelt nothing mains
Plant a dancing squirrel in the tasteful desert
Upset the single source coffee with honesty
Lace the tipples wit belly laughs. And smile.
Free us from the fragrant's stale breath

And if we can't,
If there's no way free from
Polite purgatory

Kiss me in the hallway with living passion
Slide your hand places with provocation
Shake, disrupt, break these gendered grouplets
Take fresh forays of illicit flirtation
Beneath the tasteful tablecloth drapery
Smoke with the flamboyance of an open door
Just don't ask for the recipe of anything. Ever
Fuck it all, drink what you like – gin with the fish
Scorn Radiohead, show your love of Miley. Little Mix.
Toss away the canapés, fuck in the kitchen,
Text me filth between courses
We'll chew on this gristle, but in this mannered night
We remain alive in the underground.

Falls

If they weren't here,
If sun dappled through trees
To glint on limestone boulders
In gentle peace,
Water rushed in urgency
Over nothing more than
A dipper's bobbing legs,

Then, oh then,
In the silence of the
Relentless cascade
Pool tumbling, blanche,
Cool, a playful temptation -
I'd be unburdened, weightless
This afternoon
Not corner nooked, tethered.

Fruit Bowl

Pale flesh beneath a skirt of dark peel,
Revealingly rent! A twist of
Thin white pith protecting inner
Succulence. Juicy, ripe; but not my tea.

Easy in fruit bowl sat, nestling, tempting:
My gaze alights, but never, seemingly
Never, do I reach forward for you:
Tempting, delicious, untouched.

Widening the rent, tugging pith away,
Fingers juiced fluid forgiving flesh.
Segments separated; tangy sweetness
A delicate explosion on my tongue.

Thrown Words

Ah, these lovely people. Loitering in bold insecurity, ready to attempt to enforce their little vision of heteronormative beigeness at every turn. at every turn. they've been with me pretty much as long as I can remember, back to primary school days. Back then there was the danger I might be a 'pansy', exhibited 'Nancy-boy' tendencies in not liking sport. there was the possibility of being some sort of queer as a result of reading the Guardian, being vegetarian, liking books and Bronski Beat. The certainty, backs against the walls boys, that there was a 'bumboy' in the vicinity when I was defending gay rights as well as the miners/ (Dear me. A commie as well). Oh, and I sit wrong. That's been with me for over forty years now, you'd think I'd have learnt to sit like a man by now...

They emerge, conciliatory, they haven't got a problem, don't mind your sort... No, not at all. But why - that head to toe look in slow motion, nails, shoes, something - why, why, do you have to ram it down our throats? Just saying. No offence mate. Live and let live - but not like you.

I've laughed them off, ignored them, done my thing and made a virtue of not being them. It is tiring though, and like with sport, you start to self-police, avoid things, consider (only consider mind) toning things down occasionally. Largely I tend to see them as a provocation, a call to glam up a little more, and as part of my challenge this year of exploring my journey in verse, it seemed important to bring these delights into focus.

They are insidious, annoying but harmless mostly, but they also throw eggs. and punches. they scare and intimidate people into shadows and closets and their ludicrousness needs challenging. This particular section is almost all personal, writing these has sometimes been quite draining as I've tried to get a balance between narrative distance, anger and pain Plus a certain fear about airing them.

I think it's important they don't get to sidle away though.

You are male, masculine. Manly.
A man.
The golden curls, the red sweater,
The unknowing childish enquiry of '77
cannot be,
Cannot be more than a memory
An anecdote
Ah, the staunch manliness of
anecdote
Hone your stiff upper in anecdote

Young man...
Let me tell you a tale
To cover your
Woes
(feelings)
Take a moment's silence
Dress
In monotones of middle ground
Feel the
Strength
Of timber, not the brush of the
Weeping
Beech, nor, heaven forbid, the flight
Of the playful squirrel...

Boy

Are you a girl? How often?
No fucking pansies in my house
You need the right toys
Learn you right, manliness
Isn't painted in pints of varnish

Isn't a veneer, toughen up Boy...

Boy. More? Shadow. Sheepdog. Mummy's boy. It's
the insolence of you Boy A bonfire of doll's house
shadows Cry? Cry! Cry. I'll give you something to
cry about Boy You need to learn Boy about how the
world works Hairs on your chest
I'll give you something to cry about
Up at six My father shoes that gleam Boy Pick your
nose the right way – pinky up there that's the way
Hands out of pockets Boy

No softness in the tear-drop undulation of emotion,
Living in polished dovetail timber boxes

Red polo neck at seven, the question asked
Of the blond curls
The innocence of a spark ignited
Slow burning through the decades
Tinder glowing in the emotive undergrowth
Of the lingeringly unspoken
Glowing in the headlong cornered rush
Of a darkly cornered hedonistic kiss
But. Boy.
Boy.
The artifice crumbles from archaic anecdote
The performative vacuum
Wheezes across decades and
Boy standing in pansy strewn ashes
The blazing doll's house impossibility
Reduced to the dark dance
Of sullen pints
Silent pints
Naught said
Silences

A boy's glittering soul glinted forever
-            No Boy. No.
Through tears, through silence, through barbs
Ridicule, banter, every fear, just teases
Through
And
I am not Boy, not he, but
Dancing, tearful, over-sensitive
Fearful, thrilled, silent, loud, glittered
Agonised, delighted
Skipping
A delirious cacophony of cavorting
Planting the borders of that doll's house's echoes
With flamboyant bedding
Relishing
Questions.
Boy.

As Mike did say,
            What a bunch of fist-fuckers.
Dribbling diatribes of hate,
            Drooling with lewd imaginings
            Concocting wild conspiracies
            Wailing Common-Sense
            From their putrid banter puddles.

Well, and this may be a quote,
            Fucking dick-bag arseholes.

As I read (and hear, watch, block)
            There's something else
            Some solid ground in this
                        Swamp of just-banter
bullying

These foaming ravings are
            The fulminations of the defeated;
            Their picket world of certainties
            Slipping
                        Away
            Their binary dreams of
                        Sin and sovereignty
Sliding away to the forever archive

So, they flail, clutch, scream
                        Invoke insults, threaten,
            In futility,

For these fucking fuckers –
            Like Billy Bragg's fascists,

            Are all going to lose.

A Corner

You've got eggs for your anger,
Fleet feet, eyes down and cowled;
I've got glitter, eyes that sparkle,
Heels that lift in silvered joy.

That casual disgust, tossed in venom
Might strike, shake, bring a tear,
But a sink moment, a drain's gurgle
And I'm out , pirouetting, again.

Here, there, from bar to lounge,
Track to track, these streets
Resonate with iridescent eye-liner,
Lightfooted in joyous moves.

And. Unbidden. The 2am him.

Pride

You've got regurgitated racism,
Diatribes of spoiling bile to spit:
You've got no time for my sort,
You don't want it rammed –
oh, again –
Down your throat (you never do)
Holding hands with my missus?
Well, of course, we're normal, so...

No one's trying to turn you gay,
Fuck, I was just buying a gin,
Ready to bat my dance floor lashes
When you tapped my shoulder, shared.

The joy. But, you see...

I came out alone, found my niche
Beneath the strobe, glass in smiling hand,
Feet a-flutter to endless endless beats,
Found people, my people, glittering
In kaleidoscopic smiling shards, and,

As the sun rises on us, we'll fly out, on...
Souls free on soaring sequinned waves.

Tone

Forever I've been told
        To reign it in a bit
Be a little more savvy
        Tone it down, understand
        The politics,
        Play the game.
Take the line of least resistance,
        Say yes,
        Do whatever - quietly.

Just fill in C of E
        For ease, a quiet life,
Stay under the radar
        Self-edit, just think
What would it look like?
        What will they think?
Least said, soonest mended
        After all
        And it's really best
        Not to frighten those horses.

Oh my though, I'm uncomfortable
        In the middle of the road
        Beige is not my colour
        Acquiescence not my vibe

        Frankly, fuck consensus
        The mannered, polite and
        Delicately phrased bigotry;

I'm living in the full swirling vortex
        Of life, language
        Of rainbow colour

I'm taking sides and
        Bollocks to propriety.

Unusual

I caveat a lot with the preface
I know, I'm unusual

It's even been said I'm contrary
Deliberately non-conformist. Wilful.

And, to an extent, I suppose,
There's truth on those fringes

I see no wisdom in crowds
No authority in the suit,
Tradition, custom and practice

Comfort lies beyond binaries
Outside the ossified relics
Of all that we know we know

In the radical indeterminacy
Lies freedom - to change, challenge

Discover in exploration
The thrill of understanding

And so, yes. I'm wilful, contrary
          Because how can I always learn,
          Know I'll always know nothing

Unless
          I question
          Always
          Everything?

Throat

Genuinely
I had no intention,
Not a single one,
Of ramming it down your throat.
Honestly,
I was simply minding
My own business,
Having a little chat,
Just busy on a Saturday afternoon
Doing that me thing
In the chilly spring sun,
When you jutted in angles
Intruding,
With words dredged from
Eighties darkness.
But seriously,
I doubt so very much,
So very, very much
If anyone's ever been tempted
To ram it down your throat.
Except,
Perhaps,
Your unsought thoughts.

It's fun, a bolt hole for the mind
A velveteen comfort blanket
So
Just stop

Making everything so serious,
Lighten up
It's not meant like that, it's
A bit of
Fun

But what

What

If that escape is over the wall into

The same - the same - the same

The crying pansy football sport try harder fucking man-up
Sitting like a girl some sort of queer stand properly
I'll give you something to cry about man-up
Big girl's blouse mummy's boy eh, can't take a joke

Escape? Escape into... oh. There's no
Escape
If the blanket's a thicket of thorns
Binding scarring with decades of daily

Oh stop stop stop
Stop being so over-sensitive

Daily lived disparagement

That, that, in the acrid smoke of the burning wrong toy
On the mocking breeze echoing from sport's field
That hiding beneath my bed

Escapism

That

That's no escape, no fun, no comfort

Your banter, your masculinity, your just a laugh
Are the loneliness of my solitary tears

And that's why I make it all so
Bloody serious

I'm tired
And
Can't take a joke.

Provocation

So much language in legs, not the ones
Everlasting in fevered imaginings of cliché,
But these ones, tucked inoffensively, I think,
beneath the table, neatly heels together

Functioning as legs do, supporting, balancing,
Sometimes, perhaps making statements with

skinny denim, Converse rainbows or glitter...
largely these legs are heedless, ignorant,
of their apparent reckless provocation

For yes, forty years of outrageous limbs,
Decades of blithe disregard for morality,
In these limb's folds a binary affront
Brazen offence, an incorrection,
A fiendish threat to manliness, manhood

For, terrible to say, yes, I cross my legs.
But wrong.
Tucked over neatly at the knee,
Thigh to thigh, calf against shin,
Ankle ready to fidget in rhythm
An abomination.

Rebuked, reprimanded, challenged. Told.
Desist! Cease your feminine posture,
Told, at seven, you sit like a girl
Just saying - the passing acquaintance
Banters in the bar - you sit like a woman

No offence

Flexing as I sit again, gin before me,
Preparing to lift a foot, rebellion
in the knee's touching provocation.
Just so much language in these legs.

Pool

Balls set,
An explosion of frustration
Fades into the pint of solace;
I step forth
Deftly chalking my cue,
Bending
Gliding the smooth length
Through
The crease
Soft between thumb
And forefinger,
Eye set,
Focussed...

Loosed - frustrated,
I ruse, watching the oscillation
Of ball in pocket

As

Close in my ear
He murmurs, passing and gone

"You should be on Grindr"

An Enquiry

What the fuck do you look like?
The twat asked entirely unprompted.

Taking time from valuable conformity
To demean with blithe belittling care

Thank you so much for beigeing your
Way from the middle of the road

Risking fence Verdigris on your banal jeans
The blank canvas of your tee, your mind

Obviously unwinds beyond the monochrome
Of a binary normative existence

Let me tell you, now thoroughly prompted
Just what the fuck I look like

Alive, in a fabulous shirt I love
Polished in the glitter of expression

Sipping life in skinny jeans,
Tapping tunes of delight, sparkling

With banging heels, rocking linguistic
Dreams that'll break your tiny mind.

So, dullard, I'm just busy being me,
Fabulous, insecure, so glad I'm not you.

Pink

Pink
Is the necessary provocation
The needle needed for opprobrium.
Pink
The catalyst for invective,
Nails, tee or jacket
Glitter or cord,
It's the pink gets them going.
Perhaps, maybe, my
Pink
Threatens their beige days
Nights, thoughts. Thoughts?
Really, though, just how
Secure
Is your manly masculinity
If a single top
Pink
In the casual weekend dark
Enrages, confuses, emasculates.
Perhaps, maybe you should
Think, sparkle,
Reach for your inner
Pink.

People

The Glitter of a Big Cock

Glitter of a Big Cock
Strolling by, homeward, it's 4am,
There's the echoes of funk
Of gin, Princess Bombs, tequila,
Playing tag with pre-dawn smiles.

Ahead, a couple sway in tipsy affection,
All hands, wobbling pauses
And careful stepped corrections.

Passing, there's a moment, a glance
A complicity in nights well lived,
Of heels, fedoras and moves made.
A smile, a word and he says

With gaze traversing sequins
Glitter heels, iridescent eye-liner

As I change pace,
Tapping Holly Johnson
Back to still dancing ears,
Getting a playful slap for his thoughts
He says
You must have a fucking huge cock,
To dress like that.

Russet

Gallivanting in the pockets of your mind
Moments of time a tonic of dreams,
Gregarious whims broken on circumstances
Outcrops of resolutely rocky silence.

Dance with me in late night yearning
Walk with me through the late hours
Linger late with thoughts, midnight talk,
Stray with me through the flirting hour,

Oh, you abstract thought, bar tempting
In skinnies, in smiles, in beards, in wishes.
Oh, dally in my mind late and carefree
Unheeding, thoughtless and silently departing.

You, my friend, my unknowing gorgeous
friend,
Soft folds of tended russet upon your chin,
Waft lust like laughter in your gin sips
And I, cushioned by yearning, think. Think.

Yes.
Another.

Otter

Cavorting in smooth furred grace
Rolling in gentle playfulness

Curling with inquisitive litheness
Through the undergrowth of my mind

Thickly firm tail directing these games
With practiced powerful strokes

Gliding, front and back, head cocked
Through sliding limitless games

Tumbling amid the tussocks in balls
Of smooth furred playful wonder

Nibbling, biting, leaping, darting...
Every precise arch, dart and dive

Glistens with the sheen of sunlight
Playing across firmly honed flanks

Graceful in the joy of playful turns,
Endless lithe games of firm wonder

At dusk, noon and sun's slow setting.

Please

Reach for a touch
In the silences
Brush a shoulder
When eyes dip
Fold an arm softly
Against the fears
Finger my neck
Against the tension
Say a little word
When worries whisper
Just reach out
When I crumble
Touch me with love
And in your care
Warm the void within

Gardener

Deckchair dappled in laburnum shade,
Stretching in the sultry lemonade stillness,
Watching the lawn wending wheelbarrow
Roll between lushly rich verdant beds
Guided deftly by lean gardener's arms,
Snug shirt-sleeves neatly bicep rolled,
Fingers filthy with the temptation of toil
Curled firmly about the jutting handles.

Story Arc

Thinking, the flighty sort of thinking
Flitting in unexpectedly to linger with relish,
Fuck me, given half a chance I would...

Café

This illicit coffee steams in thought
By the thrice bitten pastry,
Sitting in spiced fruit temptation
Moist creases spiral succulent shadows
As beneath the table hands stray for crumbs
Along denim snug December thighs
And wishes whisper eye to eye
With the daring finger's subtle brush
The whisper is perhaps lip soft for more,
Another bite, a nibble, a lingering eye caught sip,
An invitation laid, accepted, in the lust
Of urgently squeezing tips
Rising, a tryst in lingering desires warms
Thoughts and steps, sultana rich
Shared on lips resonant with longing
For the tastes of an afternoon dipping
Into the dusky heart of yearning.

Procrastination

Thoughts dissipate in the rain
washed away in an afternoon,
Ideas drifting in the steam of coffee
Forgotten in sips of eavesdropping

Characters loiter, nonchalant
On the neglected brow of ambiguity
Uncaptured moments gutter drift
Off and away with fag end splashes

All these hours stretch behind
Littered with inky intent's silhouette

Stairs

Over, done, finished.
The tears and words dried
That slow stretching of us
Snapping you and me into two.
There've been sobs, new rooms,
Sympathy and movie nights
And now, as friends and grown-ups
There's our gig, anticipation gig,

Tickets of alternative times when...
As friends though, adults, yes. Lets.

So in the dark, with the lights
The throb, the beat, the bass lines
And drums and lyrics shared
In this sweating tumult of bodies
In the leaping joy of this night,
Our bodies slide in proximity,
Timeless fragments of tough
Sheen our rhythmic midnight hedonism
Cocoon us as we stumble, taxi giggle
In a warmth of exhilaration. And kiss.

The driver's seen it all of course,
But we as one, one last time,
On that early hour back seat ride
Does he see my straying hand?
Your wrapping exploring hand?
The swift clasp gasp flick?
Does he spy the denim buttons
Unhooked for more? Do we care?

Tumbling in desire across the lawn
There's the gate post to press against
The wall where you free me
A step of kisses with clothes askew
Shoulder bare with bites of neck, lips...

Keys discarded, stair length too much
You push me down, less than halfway,
Work up, swallow slowly, swiftly
Tunes still giggling on your tongue tip.

I taste myself on your lips
Longing for richness to fill my mouth
But your jeans yield to the dark
And in that stepped straddle, I can
Feel as you feel my yearning
And we kiss as you reach
A press, kiss, shift, a tiny wiggle
And I'm tipped inside, slow, still
Incrementally stretching our night.

Feeling your passion in the language
Of your tongue's dance, lyrical in inches
Your beat, your tone and I follow
Every thread of improvisation
Folding, holding into you through
Crescendo and tightly wrought melody
Until, breathless, hands on every sliding
Curving arching vertebrae - I, you...

Clutching at last. One last. Our last.

In the corner of the December lit café,
Sat in the seductive skinniness of
Black jeans and playful smiles,
Legs languid across the corner sofa,
Mince pie awaiting your lip's embrace,
You're snug in the cushion's comfort,
Inviting me into the cushioning folds.

Greetings stray from fragile tentativeness
Of distances lived to intimacies,
Splayed ayes and brushed shoulders.
Soft laughter shades the movement
Of your hand across my crooked thigh;
I feel your fingers brush, furtively,
The dark denim outline of my cock.

Glancing, for a second, my eyes dip

Between your thighs, imagining, you see...
Delicately, you part your legs a little
A coffee reaching shift, so subtle, unreal,
And the curving seam's dip pulls my thoughts.

Leant conspiratorially, your finger brushes now
Your eyes widened in eyebrow challenge

My hand sliding along the dark weft...
And you cross your legs, folding me in,
Tight against the prominence of your desire
As with eyes locked, you sip your latte.

Latte

I've got pictures of you on the beach
When you were young, pictures of
Weddings and Christmases beneath
Crepe streamers and paper chains.
I have memories of rough-and-tumble,
Of dogs and sunken gardens, I remember
Conversations and you getting older,
Though I didn't notice that, you were
Just always there. Always would be.

I moved away, and while I was gone you started to go.
            You were frail and quiet at my graduation,
                                                    the
last time you left home,
except to wander to primary schools in your dressing
gown.
        You went somewhere

Strange,
                    where men live in fridges,
                                            when
they're not shooting the goldfish.
You began to throw away your past,

Confused at why people left

                                all this
  in your house.
                                            You
thought my nephew was me,
and I your sister's fancy man

                            - such a flighty thing! -

We laugh about it all, but to mask our tears,
I didn't see you enough in your failing years.
Guilt is my companion when you greet my son,
pat his giggles and think he's a dog.

Old Photographs

Shopping

As I step from my car, balancing cares on frowns,
Keys juggled in plastic bag hands, you stand
In your post-coital dressing gown, smoking stares,
Gazing unblinking, unsmiling, at my banality.
Behind you he tweaks his towelling robe, ignored,
While you lift your cigarette past your cleavage,
Leaning nonchalant against the door jamb,
Bare feet, bare legs, bare eyes that challenge.
My glance drops at your sober Sunday glare,
Knowing you stand in loosely tied Marlboro Lights
Daring me to know you're barely sated
By this rented front door, and soon you'll dress.
Covering yourself lightly in late afternoon ease,
Popping to the corner shop as you make tea
To pick up a loaf, milk and make smile contact;
Our knowledge prominent still as we queue.

Eye Contact

The silent meal of the straight couple -
He gazing over her shoulder
Watching the drifting street
She, elbow leant, sighing,
Catching the lingering eye
Of a tipsy teapot.

Heads turn to
But eyes
Are magnets set
North to north

And

She sighs, shifts,
As he
Accommodating the waiter
Smiles
Lifts his phone,
Swipes for the score.

Sigh.

Ten minutes now.

Eyes

Ah, you tell me you couldn't write
But words cascade from your smile
And in the cadence of your tales
I feel the story you have to tell.

In the depths of a long-held gaze,
The curl of cheek free hair,
I see your story unfolding
Lingering in complexity
As the night yawns, stretches,
Stands still and listens for you.

And ah, you do not need to write,
For eyes hold your tales
In the melody of your smile;

Ah, eyes, such eyes, your story...

Fields

You're not moving
Because he moved on

Left those northern dreams
To crash around you

Standing in bare fields
Of a shrugged midwinter

A Flint's Spark

Wisps of memory sting the eyes
As that Madness song plays when it oughtn't;
You try to light up in defence,
But the wheel just grazes you thumb,
For the flint's spark's reticence taunts you.
Foot to the floor, you pass her road again,
Unturning despite every sinew yearning
For a dash up the tiled path, a smiling door
Opening to picnics, one more woodland stroll.
Instead you try and recall the fading night,
When those seconds at the back gate
Were everything for two, not a solitary thought
Choking you on the Great North Road.
The road's spray disguises your desperation
In relentless concentration on the now;
Somewhere near her leaking Converse splash,
Her smile breaking someone's gloom,
As, on the flip side, your smoke catches,
And away south again, memory stings the eyes.

The Way Home

Midnight brick cold against your arse,
Back grazing acid crumbled stone
The chill of winter's decay
Scraping cold pressed skin in the dark
Miserable light seeping in pallid torpor
From midnight thoroughfare's revelry,
Fly adrift as cracked cast iron
Dripping drainpipe in desire's darkness
Hard sucked into night's rich beard
On darting waves of tongued temptation
A gin spasm of liquid late year lust

1
Longing knelt and deeply taken
2
Unzipped shadows
3
Seconds of slippery yearning
4
Unseen, unheard, heard, fully known

Kissing the residue of Friday night discourse
From urgent lips, pulled buttock tight
The moment draining droplet quick in time
Tidied quickly with kisses they step
In hands back to the sodium light
Of promises still to come

Growth

Drifting Road

Passing through the winds of lanes
And ways
This road through the woods drifts
In thought
Takes a sideways detour unexpected
To the coast
Where waves wash scoured puddles
And wind
Diverts this drifting road far inland
To hills
Rich with rocks of hidden green vales
Nestling
In the vagary of an ambling byway's
Capricious whimsy
Tramp this road through dell and field
Pause
In summer tranquillity beneath gnarled yew
And breath
The possibilities of coasts, hills, forests,
Marshes rich
With birdsong and the chatter of chance
That takes
This drifting road to your door and on
Somewhere.

Sweet Paradox

Set in fluid stone
I know exactly what I want,
Endlessly changeable, thrilling
With novelty
Yet, oh, sweet paradox,
I have played these days
Picture perfect in my director's eye,
Know well the moods,
The nuances, the perfection
That ought to be found
In this freeform unplanned day.
I feel the artist's disappointment
As I lay down the brush
Forever unable to accept
Vision and reality, sometimes,
Just cannot match.

Edging

A lifetime spent making virtues of edges,
Stood watching in comforting shadows,
Relishing the fringes from alcoves,
Watching the beautiful people in all
Their strange, terrifying, confidence;
Leant on sweaty walls in fearful corners
Building my acquaintance niche
Of skulking gregarious isolation.

And I stood in the dark of decades
Yearning, fearing the movement of arms;

Disturbed by the thought of dance...
Hiding discomfort in dismissal -
so shallow, my roll-neck cynicism so cool
and yet, brushed pooling eyes hide
a tap, a hidden twitch in stilled hips.

Now, here I am, again. In strobe aloft,
On a wave of funk-soul drum-n-bass grime,

Now though, I long to be there, in the midst
The middle, glitter queening, dressed in gin

Now, yeah, absolutely, I'll attention whore -
And proud - I've bid farewell to those edges.

Revelation

Did I, taking his penis in my mouth
Behind Kwik Fit
Secure in the wheelie bin's arms
Know?
Well, maybe, but I was distracted
And there was alcohol, so...

It could be the lingering kiss
Against the sweaty wall
Was a give-away, but then again,
There were beers and youth and
After all
Everyone explores...

Or, the man with the clipped moustache
Who asked, up close,
Does my 'tache make your testicles
Tingle...
Oh, but that was only yesterday,
So...

Maybe, but fuck, just so many
A mind filled, top and bottom
With possibles
Should have, could have, I did know
Long before I opened my lips
For his penis.

Another Rainy Day

Bereft, these days linger again,
refracting shades of grey,
puddled streets reflecting nothing
In the sodium rippled sheen

A year since your
last cloud break smile,
when for one northern day
we, briefly, shone again.

You're receding, silence weaving,
intonations of amusement a myth,
your silliness hazier by the day,
even pain's terseness now misting.

Where once you taught me
the true use of puddles,
Rain falls in terraced rivulets,
of what once we were.

Leading me on streets in holed Converse,

frolicking in flowing hands... but,
Pavement skies hold their gloomy grip,
Hiding the glittering shards of days:

I shall though step outside,
giggle at all the tomorrows,
and splash in memories:
you taught me puddle's meaning

Back To Life

Cascading rough and tumble giggle of
Red roll necked blonde curls,
He clambers across the rockery's years
With tears for the passing of Puff,
Light with laughter in the endless sun
Even as the doll's house ashes drift away

He's always on the corner, waiting,
Searching for the promised
Sale of discount dreams
Wishing for an iridescent touch
Wishing for one shimmering song

Dark with the loneliness of party tears,
Standing alone in the fashioned shadows
Staring out, building haughty walls
Though he's just sultry, interesting,
Channelling that Jimmy Dean poster
In the vindictive nightclub corner

He's always on the corner, waiting,
Searching for the promised
Sale of discount dreams
Wishing for an iridescent touch
Wishing for one shimmering song

Dreaming of Metroland, always,
he's in the knotted embrace of tweed
an armoured masked safety
Loitering long with the solace of rage
His anger capped with wishes the world
Would linger with him just once

He's always on the corner, waiting,
Searching for the promised
Sale of discount dreams
Wishing for an iridescent touch
Wishing for one shimmering song

Silence blankets him, nothing's safety
Hiding in fantasy behind lips sealed stiff
The wishes of passing years loft bound
He wonders, sipping autumn coffee
Where it all went, how it came the
Tumbling passed by leaving only scowls

He's always on the corner, waiting,
Searching for the promised
Sale of discount dreams
Wishing for an iridescent touch
Wishing for one shimmering song

Oh this! This! The tumbling leaf-mould
Puddle splashes of this mixing tin dash,
Hidden in dusk's hollow tangle – dreams!
Just racing with moments in the ginnel
These days light with unearthed laughter
Eyes closed In the endless dusk

He's always on the corner, waiting,
Searching for the promised
Sale of discount dreams
Wishing for an iridescent touch
Wishing for one shimmering song

Standing still, untangling the anguish
He moves, finding tentative steps unseen,
Dreams glittering again before sunrise,
The relentless optimism of a night
Well danced seizes him, and pansy soft,
Ashes of long-lost possibility drifts down

He's always on the corner, waiting,
Searching for the promised
Sale of discount dreams
Wishing for an iridescent touch
Wishing for one shimmering song

Sitting under the table's fine;
Believe me,
I still sit beneath the table
Or, on the arms of chairs
Because at my age,
Frankly, who's telling me off?

Like that walking on walls thing,
Balancing, tiptoe skip along
The curved capping of Tower Street
To jump, leap, in fear and thrills -
Flying - landing - stumbling. Upright.

That's the thing, like kicking leaves
Or heedless puddle jumping
You really need to hold those.
People always say don't,
Just so many no folk in grey.
Always someone telling you
That's not right, not the feeling
Not the thing. Just blend in. Behave.

There's the wall, another, of course.
The garage wall, by the back gate path
Where that thing, the big thing
The first (or second really -

Oh, doll's house tears, I know)

Was said and placed firmly
In thoughts that lingered
(and still do, I haven't forgotten)
That first, second, brick
Behind a hiding wall,
A sheltering, safety first, wall

Let me say, you build walls well

Forty-year walls; strong bricks,
silent mortar, bonds of hiding

Crying in the lee of knowing

When they came around that corner
On that fresh path, with the girl thing
Ah, germinating delight,
Tendrils binding, clasping, seeking
The crevices to break that wall

And, you should know this, listen,
You know your truth now,
That's the smile, the heart, the smile,
And whatever time it'll take,

A leap from those brick cappings
And, in years, you will fly. Deliciously.

Ripples

The churning rhythm of these days
Hides its turbulence beneath the
False frivolity of sombre discourse,

That spring, when every day shone,
A jeweller's year of diamond days,
Fled with the onset of summer clouds,

And with stiff lips, the shooting star's
Revealed for headlamps flashing on
A wobbling November antennae,

But just tickle the puddles in the dark,
Don the wellingtons and leap forth,
For the turbulence of ripples glitter too.

(Canute)

Repeatedly – daily –
I set myself against the tides,
Flail, rage at the radio,
Fulminate at the news.

Stand against the waves,
The lashings of language
Against my shivering knees.

So many years on this shiftless shore
Tight, bright, resolute against it all,
Not maligned Canute reimagined,
Rather Viola Wittrokiana
Blooming through late spring storms.

You

Oh yes, you.

In dreams and thoughts.

In moments.

In reality

Fantasy

Days Night Years

You

The Heat of Consent

The Heat of Consent
There's a whole thing, grumbled,
Groused, in scowling seductiveness,
That, somehow, consent's
A bit uncool, a little, well, unsexy
Just takes away that little
Frisson of, well, something.

But – oh yes, that –
I'll say – please could you –
That – no, just there –
Hearing – I like that –
Just – a little more, yes –
What – could you, oh –
Your – doing is great –
Lover – shall I just –
Wants – I'll show you –
Is just sexy as fuck

And, consent is fluid,
Slippery as desire, shifting,
Taking, giving, changeable,
As movable as horny hands,
As lust laden as lips on mine.
Melt me with seductive
Clear, explicit, wonderful,
Welcoming sexy consent.

In the light, in the dark, in the sultry spaces
Of musing imagination, dallying fantasy...
In caresses, fleeting touches and lingering kisses,
There are things you just don't believe,
Yet beneath the slumbering duvet's warmth,
On kitchen's dancing tiles and the sofa's curl,
There are a thousand things that are just true.

You have delicious thighs that tantalise,
That tempt and draw my lips for languid kisses;
Calves, lips and breasts I'd linger over for hours;
Eyelids, lashes and fingers to longingly stroke
Soft with the urgency of long dreamt desire,
Your delectable derrière calls for the squeeze of
Fingers trailing across every inch of your
Joyous body - toe, calf, breast, sex, arm, ear
Smile

And I dream, I think, I fidget in afternoon fantasy,
Evening consideration, coffee cloud thought
Of you disrobed, disrobing, a revelation
A sigh on my lips, a sigh on your skin,
A butterfly kiss of awakening,
A flutter of belief
As you realise what I know so well,
That you are everything:

Seductive.
Beautiful.
You.

Belief

At The Gig

Secure in corner's dark,
Reverberating notes lark,

Ears bouncing in strobed joy
limbs flying like toys,

I see you, breathless, leaping
grinning with the two hundred,

As, wild haired, this singer throws
himself to the tumult, the flowing,

Sparkling keyboard crescendo
lifting me to the melee's heart,

Smitten by these charms;
I'm carried headlong to your arms.

Talking

Talking
is underrated.

Wandering down wires or watching the words,
like a blanket it tucks away
worries, stills the niggles,
liquefies miles.

Stronger than a drug at easing life's hurts,
hours can be lost
inside the warmth of dancing laughs.

Talking
is overrated.

Sometimes, just sometimes, that sliding smile
that so light heartedly leaps my way
can say it
softer than a breath.

And when I can lie beside you, drowning
myself in your eyes,
the only sound out thoughts' drifting desires,
that speaks a thousand words
or more.

It's Morning

It's morning,
All spaniel eyes
And tails of possibility
And you make me smile.
There's coffee
In wreaths of steam
And moments of thought
And you make me melt.
There's sun, or rain
Or gentle mists
Over muddy hands
And damp soaked feet
And straightening to stretch
I'm just warmed
By the thought of you.
There's the night
When sleep is coming
And a smile, a hug, a thought
Is enough
To butterfly me
Through the night
With dreams that just delight

Christmas Shower

Adorned by glittering, dashing droplets
You are unwrapped in the shower
No coy teasing, you turn to my gaze
Hands revelatory in a slow chest slide,
My eyes traversing your litheness
Provocative eyes playing with mine,
Erect in boisterous challenge
Playful eyebrows issue their command;
Slowly on gossamer tinsel strands of lust
I kneel in the sparkling cataract
Run hands light with glittering desire
Along, up, your thighs, across
Delve into your belly-button's innuendo

grasp your buttock's arc, exploring...

Your eye's yearning pulls me closer,
Moves me into you, your gaze commanding
run my tongue compliant in firm exploration
dancing across, darting, dipping exploring
in dreams of running moments
the flushed festival of your desire.
Guiding hands grasp my head in direction,
the inverse echoes of my fervency
a surging press against insistent fingers,
you pull me to your seductive gleaming body
the cascade of our kisses washing our skin
our lips sharing the richness of our early gift.

My head will turn
I'll be drawn, oh I will
On a summer's day,
I'll be intrigued, imagine...
My eye will wander...

I fancy you, oh yes,
Ankles, thighs, lips, sexy lobes;
Oh, you fill my thoughts
Hour through hour
With all the sauce, filth,
You can possibly imagine.

I may even put those words
Somewhere.

Will I feel, leap, jump?
My desire's in hugs, in
The embrace of a movie's arms,
A kiss at the sink, a snoozing spoon,
A desire rising in
The latency of a kissed smile.

Oh, but hold me, kiss me, look
At me
Like that;
Press your tongue, caress my soul,
(sorry, arse)
And fuck me...
(please)
My desire rides piggy-back
Feeding with urgency from yours -
Lust for me
And, fuck me, I want you.

Desire

If You...

If you'd just say don't touch me
There
But there, just there
To lean into my touch by the sink
Reach for my
When I pass the sofa
Perhaps slide your fingers
Beneath the snug fringes of
A t-shirt you randomly untucked on the stairs
Tell me yes I like those soft
Kisses along neck, ears, thighs

You could always touch me there,
By the sink, on the sofa, on the lowest stair
Kiss me behind the ear, stroke my bum
And I could _
While the kettle boils and tea brews
Stroke my back in lingering finger swirls
Fingers finding vertebrae one by one
And where should I

_ _ _ _ _ _ _ _ _ _ _ _ _ _ _ _ _ _ _
If you nuzzled my neck with your warm
Breath, insistent lingering collarbone lips
_ _ _ _ _ _ _ _ _ _ _ _

You'll make me come if you do that...
Fingers insistent in dark spirals
As nipples pucker in anticipation
For the nibbling, too much, kiss

A slowing, an avoiding, a hinting,
Flirting with intensity's yearning
For slippery electric, unavoidable, touch
Sliding, away, back, over, under. Again.

That cupping, pressing tease, swift to
Long reach depths... now. Please!
The thrumming invitation accepted
On the spread of threshold fingers

Slow, soft and bold, the very gasp of yes
Without the cease of sighs subsiding
Of eyes whispered opening
Of the in-me-now tugging

A spreading, teasing, frustration
Resistant against the buttock pulling
Thigh wide taut heat of slow release
Until your depths tingle twenty toes

Of fervency, of arm-thigh entanglement
Of descending again to bite at lust
Of collarbones, tongues and fingernails –
Just fucking come in me, with me. That.

Now.

Now

Moorland

Out across the moor, over an hour,
Through thickets of gorse and bracken,
Skirting the herds, hopping brooks,
Feet unhurried rising through July hours.

Untroubled by soft summer showers,
Walking on with damp glitter in our hair,
Embracing this warm monsoon,
We skip breathless, puddle jumping from
Soggy tussock to saturated grassy mound,
Until in a crescendo if giggles we land
Beneath the dripping beech fingers.

Soaked. Shirts, socks, jeans, clinging
Like laughter, heedless with pleasure
We turn against the truck's smoothness,
Feeling the slipperiness beneath wet hands
As we kiss in sliding folds of second skin.

And still the rain comes across our shoulders,
We kiss, washed by the passion of the rain,
Hands on arses, beneath shirts, grazed by rain,
Fingers unfurling tight waistband buttons
Pressing moisture from between us,
Our liquid form fitting skin
Gathering the drops of our finger slide.

"Fuck me now," in the rain, and we
Yielding to the steep slope's pull,
Rain pounding the thirsty grass, to lie,
Folding the wet blades beneath our desire,
Our nakedness massaged beneath the cascade
Sodden clinging clothes asunder,

We slip between each other's thighs
Hands held high, feeling the welcome,
The warmth of sliding lust, skin kissed,
As the squalls pass over unheeded.

The goosebump thrill of soaked clothing
Welcomes the guttural thrust of entrance,
On the breeze, a desire of command
Just a fuck. Now. And legs fold in direction

Pulling deeper, no teasing here
In the pounding rain's driving urgency;
Neither of us yearn for this tryst's
Lingering extension, thrusting together
To come in hot urgent tumultuous waves.

And, pocketing underwear, we pull
Each other upward, walk, sodden, sated,
Ready to disrobe the moment the
Front door swings closed on the storm.

The Way Home

Midnight brick cold against your arse,
Back grazing acid crumbled stone
The chill of winter's decay
Scraping cold pressed skin in the dark
Miserable light seeping in pallid torpor
From midnight thoroughfare's revelry,
Fly adrift as cracked cast iron
Dripping drainpipe in desire's darkness
Hard sucked into night's rich beard
On darting waves of tongued temptation
An gin spasm of liquid late year lust

1
Longing knelt and deeply taken
2
Unzipped shadows
3
Seconds of slippery yearning
4
Unseen, unheard, heard, fully known

Kissing the residue of Friday night discourse
From urgent lips, pulled buttock tight
The moment draining droplet quick in time
Tidied quickly with kisses they step
In hands back to the sodium light
Of promises still to come

Please

Reach for a touch
In the silences
Brush a shoulder
When eyes dip
Fold an arm softly
Against the fears
Finger my neck
Against the tension
Say a little word
When worries whisper
Just reach out
When I crumble
Touch me with love
And in your care
Warm the void within